KNOW THE BASICS TO PROTECT YOUR BUSINESS

Robert Strickland

How do you detect **Internal Theft**?

Which **Alarm System** is best for your **Business**?

How do you protect your **Inventory**?

We show businesses how to handle:

- Dishonest Employees
- Safety Inspections
- Inventory Control
- Accident Reporting
- Building Security
- Shoplifting

http://www.besecureandsafe.com

I dedicate this book in loving memory to:

Mildred JoAnn Strickland

&

Elvira Torres Washington

I thank them for their love, encouragement
and for providing me with the
strength to overcome my fears
and to never give up the faith.

Acknowledgments

*I would like to recognize
the following individuals
for assisting me with the creation of this book.*

*My business partner and friend Ray Glaze,
my mentor Diallo "Abe" Bennett,
my coach Tom Roan,
my visionary Bill Davis,
my spiritual brethren Bill Brigham,
my guide Marna Friedman,
my sister Tanya Betton,
my aunt Angelus Rowe,
Norm Smith, Charles Dill, Cheryl Monroe,
Robert Henle, Randy Rodebaugh,
Byron Palmer, Justin Anderson, Yaminah Ahmad,
Wendy Wasley, Tosca Lamback,
Cassandra Wilson and
special thanks to David Washington
for his dedication
and sacrifice to assist me with the
preparation of this book.*

*To my family:
Pamela, Courtney & Jarett,
I love all of you so much.
Thank you for allowing me to be your foundation.*

CONTENTS

ROBERT STRICKLAND

After receiving numerous athletic scholarships to play collegiate football, Rob Strickland elected to attend North Carolina A & T State University where he starred as an all-conference linebacker.

He completed his undergraduate studies and received a Bachelor of Arts degree in Psychology. He played professional football for a short time and finished his career with the New York Jets.

Rob joined Macy's (the largest retail store in the world) Security department at Herald Square on 34th street in New York City. He moved through the ranks of Store Security Guard, Security Detective, Investigator, Assistant Security Manager, Senior Security Manager, District Security Manager, Regional Director of Investigations and Regional Vice President of Security.

Rob also managed several different markets within the organization including Florida, Georgia, Baltimore, New York, Washington, New Orleans, New Jersey, Alabama, South Carolina and Puerto Rico. His responsibility included managing the most "high-profile" events including; The Macy's Thanksgiving Day Parade, The Macy's 4th of July Fireworks, The 1996 Centennial Olympics in Atlanta Georgia & the Lighting of The Great Tree at Lenox Square Mall. He has provided security protection for numerous celebrities, entertainers and athletes. He was also responsible for the complete Security supervision of Macy's first off shore store in San Juan Puerto Rico. During his tenure with Macy's, Rob became very proficient in Alarm System Installation, Burglar & Fire Alarm Protection, Camera Installation & Surveillance, Secure Lock Devices, Safety Protection and Investigations. While at Macy's he was the recipient of numerous awards and recognition for his contribution, service and accomplishments. He produced outstanding shortage reduction results for the company on a consistent basis. He successfully served Macy's for over 22 years and protected billions of dollars worth of assets, millions of customers and thousands of employees.

As the CEO, President & Founder, and newly published author, Rob Strickland now brings his resources, experience and expertise to Strickland Security and Safety Solutions LLC.

Education & Credentials:
- Bachelor of Arts, Psychology
- Certified Diversity Trainer
- Threat Assessment Training by Secret Service, GBI & FBI
- Workplace Violence Training & Certification
- Firearms Safety & Marksmanship Certification
- Wicklander & Zulawski Interviewing & interrogations
- Gang task Force training GA Dekalb Police Department
- Bomb Detection Training
- Self Defense & Martial Arts Trained
- First Aid/Adult CPR Certified

INTRODUCTION

I n today's society there is an increasing need for people to feel secure and safe in both their place of work and home. With crime on the rise coupled with a challenging financial climate, our mission is to provide sound security and safety training, education, advice, and services to companies, businesses and individual clients in order to protect their physical and material assets. Using our expertise and knowledge of the **BASIC** principals (**B**uilding Security, **A**pprehensions, **S**afety, **I**nventory Control, & **C**ommunication), our emphasis is on helping our customers and businesses build a secure and safe foundation which would provide them the comfort and peace of mind throughout each day.

This guide is intended to educate, prepare and protect you in order to make your business more secure, safe and profitable. This guide will reinforce industry standard best practices and provide you with the needed tools to make your business successful. The training techniques described in this guide have been studied, practiced and proven successful through decades of Security, Safety and Loss Prevention experience.

BUILDING SECURITY

CHAPTER 1
BUILDING SECURITY

One of your primary functions will be to protect your business or company's assets, employees and customers. In addition, providing outstanding customer service is the number one deterrent to shoplifting, and must be viewed as a priority. To accomplish these objectives, you must be prepared to respond to theft activity, conduct building safety inspections, perform Loss Prevention audits and ensure inventory control compliance. The responsibilities discussed in this section are the **BASIC** objectives for most retail companies and businesses, but may vary depending upon assignment or business. Listed below are the typical responsibilities associated with this approach.

• Customer service

- Detect & apprehend shoplifters
- Detect & apprehend dishonest employees
- CCTV monitoring
- Safety inspections
- Inventory control audits
- Building security
- Alarm monitoring
- Accident Reporting
- Opening/closing building

Retailers and most business owners understand the importance of placing a high priority on the physical security of their buildings. In the past, retail stores exclusively invested their time into handling shortage problems and theft issues that occurred during business hours. Criminal activity has evolved and after hour break-ins and robberies are becoming more frequent. To remain one step ahead of these current problems, it is essential to not only have a well-educated and trained management team, staff or security department, but also to have a means of physically protecting the premises. This protection should consist of **BASIC** security practices and procedures in conjunction with an alarm system in order to ensure the integrity of your building or place of business. Security experts agree that prevention must be your number one strategy in fighting shortage problems or theft related issues. All buildings must be equipped with the proper locking mechanisms for doors and windows. The alarm system should be supplied and installed by a licensed alarm company with a central monitoring station. Lights must provide optimum visibility, both inside and out, with outside lighting having vandal-proof covers over the lights and power sources. Your entire perimeter must be well-lit, especially around doors and other possible entries.

Keys must be controlled. A master key system where one key opens all locks may be convenient, but it may not be the best for security purposes. The only keys that can

be taken home should be controlled by assigned key carriers. Code all keys, keep them securely locked when not in use, and do not allow employees to leave them lying around or make duplicates. Change locks whenever you suspect that key controls have been compromised or keyholder staffing changes have occurred.

ALARM SYSTEMS

Most companies and businesses invest in alarm systems for protection, so understanding alarm system capability is very important. An alarm system is needed by every business and may be required by insurance companies regardless of the size of the property. The good news is it also provides an additional layer of security. Knowing the different types of alarm systems will absolutely be necessary to alert you of fire, smoke or an intruder. In addition, an alarm system will decrease chances of a burglary. Alarm systems may reduce insurance costs or allow client to raise deductibles, which should then be used to calculate net costs for alarm systems.

In today's world most businesses are the victims of false alarms. The common practice is to consider an alarm false if there is no evidence of illegal entry or attempted forced entry. It is estimated that 80 to 98 percent of all after-hour alarm breaks are false. This has become a serious problem for police departments and a huge inconvenience for businesses.

BREAKDOWN OF COMMON ALARMS

You should consider using the following devices to protect your building:

MAGNETIC CONTACTS

If the door is open it will break the magnetic contacts connecting the door, frame or windows. When this happens, alarm activation occurs. Contacts are also used on safe doors to protect valuable merchandise such as jewelry or even cash.

MOTION DETECTORS

A motion detector responds to movement and protects interior areas, hallways and will activate when someone enters the area. For anyone who is responding to alarm activation, you need to be informed which area the motion covers and how many different motions have been activated.

Glass Breaks

Some companies use glass break sensors, which activate when glass is broken. Glass breaks work by detecting the sound and/or vibration of breaking glass.

Sirens, Strobes and Horns

Sirens and strobes are designed to make a loud audible noise with bright, flashing lights. Once the intruder hears the alarm, he/she may then quickly exit the building. They also help direct the police where the intruder may have entered.

Burglar Alarm Tests and Inspections

Testing your alarm systems is a very important component of protecting your building. If it is determined that any one of the alarm points are not operational, a call to your alarm company should be made to schedule a technician for repairs.

Routine tests and inspections of the alarm system should be conducted on a regular basis. Prior to conducting the testing, you should notify your alarm monitoring center that you are conducting an alarm test. Next, obtain a copy of your building's alarm points of protection. After this is complete, you should follow the steps listed.

1. Using your keypad, place the alarm system on test.
2. Open every exterior customer door. Walk directly beneath the motion detectors making sure you trigger the sensors.
3. Compare all alarm point activations to the alarm panel.
4. All alarm tests must be documented.

PERIMETER AND INTERIOR ALARM

Perimeter alarm protection primarily consists of contact alarms installed on all customer doors, windows, fire exits and roof hatches, or other access points. Interior alarm protection is essential in fully protecting your building. Motion detectors strategically placed throughout your building will give you maximum protection in the event that someone does gain access or remains hidden in your building.

FIRE ALARM SYSTEMS

Fire alarm protection for most buildings is a Federal/State requirement. Testing fire alarm systems is also mandatory and should be conducted by an alarm technician and/or an engineering staff or trained personnel. It is also a Federal/State mandate that all businesses have fire exit signs posted and clearly visible to alert

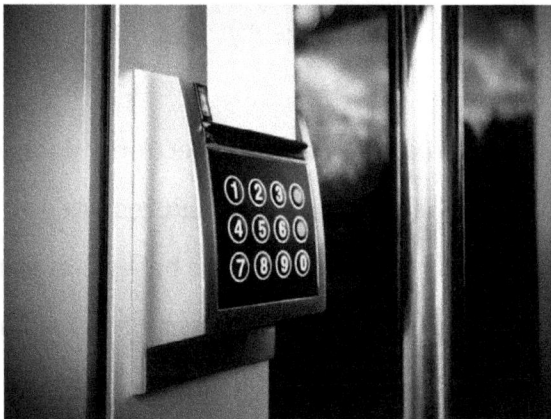

customers where to exit in the event of an emergency. Fire exits can never be blocked with merchandise, fixtures or debris.

DOOR ACCESS CONTROL

Prior to store operating hours it is recommended that you have a salesperson, security or management monitor your employee entrance. Their primary function will be to check employee's IDs. For visitors/vendors they will have to produce a photo ID and sign the logbook. Having individuals sign in lets you know how many people are in your building, which is important to know in case of an emergency.

You could also have an electronic door access control device, which would require an access card to open the door. The benefits of using access control surveillance systems are that you can automatically deter, grant, and track access to your building. There are many benefits to using this type of technology. You can now leave the door unmanned and issue access control cards to all your employees. The system can lock doors and trigger cameras while alerting police or security personnel of emergencies. Additional functions can include time and attendance monitoring, specific access only capability and a detailed activity report.

CLOSED CIRCUIT TELEVISION

Another cost-effective way to protect your company or business is to invest in a Closed Circuit Television (CCTV) security system. This is the

most popular method used by businesses. CCTV helps to protect your business and employees; it is a visible deterrent against theft and vandalism. CCTV footage can be invaluable in the identification and prosecution of perpetrators of crimes.

The benefits to the installation of CCTV systems are both numerous and practical:

1. Reducing potential insurance claims.

2. Increasing staff productivity.

3. Identifying criminals.

4. Monitoring high shortage areas with poor visibility.

5. Deters theft, malicious mischief and vandalism.

6. Unlimited monitoring and surveillance.

YOU BECOME THE ALL-SEEING EYE WITH CCTV

For anyone using a CCTV security system you must have an understanding of what it can do and how to properly utilize all of its capabilities. With the evolution of technology you can now monitor your business or home from a remote location. This represents the latest technology in Closed Circuit Television. There are two schools of thought related to CCTV monitoring:

*   Assign staff to monitor your cameras which will give you real time video footage.

*   Use a digital video recorder (DVR) to monitor a specific area and review later or when there is a need.

BREAKDOWN OF COMMON VIDEO EQUIPMENT:

- Digital Video Recorder (DVR)
- Covert Camera
- Remote Monitoring/IP Cameras

DVR

With the advancement of technology DVRs are now the preferred method of recording. In the past most companies used VCR tapes with the recording capability between 8 to 72 hours. Digital video recorders (DVRs) give you a higher resolution, data memory of 30 days or more, and most have a remote monitoring network built-in. In addition all video images are stored on the hard drive in a digital format.

COVERT CAMERA

Covert cameras can be invisible to the general public and used to discreetly detect employee theft and shoplifting. Some covert cameras are wireless while others require direct cable connections. Covert cameras should be installed in an area where they cannot be detected*.

REMOTE MONITORING/IP CAMERAS

IP network cameras send live video streams via digital packets across an IP network such as a LAN (Local Area Network) or Internet. IP cameras give businesses increased flexibility because you can monitor them remotely and store the data.

Special Note: Fitting Rooms – There is a legal expectation of privacy involving fitting rooms and there can be absolutely no camera recording of any kind. Make sure cameras are only used in common areas.

BUILDING EMERGENCY PROCEDURAL TIPS

What is considered an emergency? An emergency is any occurrence of an event, which may endanger or threaten to endanger the safety or health of any person or which destroys damages or threatens to destroy or dam-

age property. The September 11, 2001 attacks alerted all companies to prepare their buildings for emergency situations. Buildings that have the necessary emergency procedures in place stand a better chance of overcoming emergency situations than those who do not. It is not a matter of if, but when an emergency will happen and you need to know how to respond. Having a complete understanding of your company's emergency procedures is critical. If there is a need to evacuate your building due to a fire or power failure, following emergency procedures can make the difference between safety and injury. It is recommended that emergency manuals are updated, read and maintained regularly. An emergency control plan should consist of advance planning, conducting simulated drills, training, testing of all equipment and properly coordinating all activities with local law enforcement officials. Do your employees know what to do if there is a power failure, bomb threat, fire, or armed robbery? Not having an updated emergency manual or employees untrained to handle a crisis can be a big mistake. To ensure that your building is secure and safe you should have the following systems in place:

- Communication process
- Fire and safety procedures
- Bomb threat procedures
- Evacuation plan
- An emergency checklist
- Sign off form by employees to confirm everyone has read and understand the emergency procedures.

COMMUNICATION PROCESS

In the event of an emergency it should be noted that a high level of communication is key. Having access to an emergency call list is important as time is not on your side. During the communication process it must be known that all information should be communicated accurately and concisely. Any information that is inaccurate or false can hurt efforts to bring a dangerous situation to a safe conclusion.

FIRE & SAFETY PROCEDURES

Large buildings present a difficult challenge for fire fighters; luckily, it is a federal mandate for all large buildings to be equipped with sprinkler systems. In addition, the Occupational Safety Health Administration (OSHA) safety standards require that all buildings have fire extinguishers. They should be located in areas of the building that are immediately accessible to all. In some places

it is common practice to use fire extinguishers to prop open doors, but this is a grave safety concern and should not be done. Automatic sprinkler protection is designed to discharge water instantly in sufficient density to control or extinguish a fire in its early stages. It consists of water discharge devices (sprinkler heads), one or more reliable sources of water at the desired pressures, valves to control the water flow, piping to distribute and convey water to the sprinklers and auxiliary equipment such as alarms and supervisory devices. There is an 18-inch vertical clearance requirement which must be treated as a horizontal plane throughout the storage area or room. All materials must be stored below this horizontal plane. The clear space between stored materials and the sprinkler deflectors allows discharge from sprinklers to overlap and pre-wet combustibles to effectively contain a fire. It is important to adhere to all local fire codes.

BOMB THREATS

Bomb threats are to be taken very seriously and can never be ignored. It is critical that you have a bomb threat plan for your building. Training of key personnel in your building is needed so they can take control to safely direct and instruct all occupants. Keep in mind that a bomb threat can be communicated to you over the phone, in writing or not at all. The most important fact to remember is not to panic and stay calm. Do not communicate the threat to the population of the building but call your local police department immediately. If it is determined that you need to look for a bomb it should be done very discretely. If you discover anything out of the ordinary do not touch it; isolate the area until the authorities arrive.

EVACUATION PLAN

Evacuating a large building with a lot of people can be a very difficult challenge. It is highly recommended that one person remains in control and directs all activity. There should be an assigned meeting place outside and all employees must be accounted for.

APPREHENSIONS/
DETERRENCE

CHAPTER 2

APPREHENSIONS/DETERRENCE

All businesses face the same problem of how to prevent customers and employees from stealing merchandise, cash and personal property. Unfortunately, not all retail companies or businesses can afford to hire store security to deter and apprehend those suspected of shoplifting or theft. In this section of the guide we will look at businesses that employ security and those who do not. We will examine how to become a security expert and successfully make internal and external apprehensions. Knowing the **BASIC**s will help you in terms of when

& how to react to a shoplifting incident. We highly recommend that you utilize our 5-step guideline for making an apprehension that has been proven successful throughout the retail loss prevention industry. This 5-step apprehension guideline is aimed at protecting the company from false detainments or customer incidents. Customer service is the number one objective for all retailers, and any incident involving security, employees and a customer can negatively impact your business and reputation. Do keep in mind that a shoplifting incident is a breakdown in customer service and employee theft is a breakdown in supervision.

Retail industry statistics reveal that 47 percent of inventory shortage is caused by employee theft. Early detection and apprehension is the key to maintaining a profitable business. After it is revealed that an employee has stolen from the company it is important to know how to approach the employee and subsequently apprehend them. It's imperative that the incident is handled in accordance to labor laws and employee rights.

Similar to the shoplifting 5-step guideline you must also follow a basic approach of having strong evidence that indicates the employee has stolen from the company.

FIVE STEP GUIDELINE TO
MAKING A SHOPLIFTING APPREHENSION

ENTRY

It is highly recommended that you see the customer enter your store or a department within your building. Based on your initial observations, you must establish that the subject did

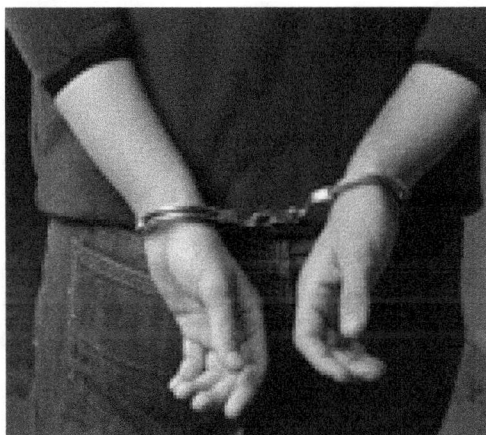

not enter your building with the merchandise to return.

SELECTION

Seeing selection of the merchandise gives you the confidence that the items belong to your company. Make a mental note of how many items and colors were selected.

CONCEALMENT

You must witness concealment of the merchandise. Watch out for the customer who decides to dump/discard the merchandise.

Special Note: Not all merchandise will be concealed. Some people will walk directly out of the building with the merchandise in plain sight.

CONTINUOUS OBSERVATION

You must maintain continuous observation of the shoplifter until he/she exits the building.

EXIT

Allow the customer to pass cash register/ wrapstand areas which confirms their desire not to pay for merchandise. For the safety of the employee and customer, the apprehension should take place near the exit door.

Special Note: Some businesses implement 25 foot curb rules in order to prevent foot chases of suspects. This means you cannot apprehend an alleged shoplifter if they are 25 feet beyond the curb.

We strongly recommend that prior to engaging in an apprehension that you thoroughly review all your company's apprehension policies and procedures. If you don't have an established policy, then contact us for assistance. We'll create one specifically for your needs.

APPREHENSION METHODS /

HOW TO MAKE SHOPLIFTING CASES

In the early years when there were no CCTV cameras in the building you had to learn how to work a case from the selling floor. This required you to develop floor surveillance skills in an effort not to be detected by the potential shoplifter. This was an effective way to make a case because you could make a case by yourself while meeting all the elements needed of a 5-step process. As the security retail industry evolved and new technology was redeveloped, CCTV became the first choice for making cases. Listed below are some helpful tips on how to successfully make an apprehension.

FLOOR SURVEILLANCE FOR SECURITY PERSONNEL ONLY

- Before going to the floor, be prepared. Have your radio, handcuffs, shopping bag, small writing pad and pen available.
- Observe a high shortage area within your store.
- Do not stand inside the department, but out of the area so your view point is wide and you can see ev-

eryone who enters the department.

- Once you have observed a suspicious customer enter the department, you will then enter the department to continue surveillance.

- Act the part of a shopper by looking at merchandise and observing the customer utilizing your peripheral vision. Do not make eye contact with the customer.

- After you see selection, make a note of the item, how many, color, quantity, etc.

- After you see concealment, you will want to move close to the nearest customer exit while still continuing your surveillance.

- Taking into consideration that you have the first four steps and the customer makes an attempt to exit the store you can now feel comfortable with making the detainment.

- Wisdom always dictates that you first identify yourself as a representative of the company and then take possession of the merchandise before escorting the shoplifter back to the security office.

CCTV FOR SURVEILLANCES AND APPREHENSIONS

CCTV cameras are a great tool for businesses to use to control theft. For starters having highly visible cameras are a big deterrent for shoplifting and employee theft. With today's technology one security person can now monitor an entire store. CCTV has made this possible, and if utilized properly, can identify a significant amount of shoplifting activity. Typical camera systems allow you to program patterns and targets. This will enable you to monitor high shortage departments and registers. Cameras that have been preprogrammed give you the opportunity to monitor your store without an operator.

AFTER SETTING UP THE CAMERAS MAKE SURE YOU:

- Know each camera location (walk to the exact location of the camera on the floor) and which departments it can see

- Understand how to program the camera system so it automatically moves to designated departments and registers

- Develop the ability to anticipate where the customer will move next and select the corresponding camera to ensure fluid and contin-

uous coverage.

- Perform regular maintenance to ensure all camera equipment is operating properly.
- Always have your cameras pointed on the hot (high shortage areas) departments
- Use your viewing monitor wisely and do not sit too close to them. Sitting back gives you a better view point and will allow you to view multiple monitors simultaneously.

Give yourself a break from watching the cameras after a couple of hours. The human eye can only watch the cameras for so long without eye fatigue.

ORGANIZED RETAIL CRIME

Organized Retail Crime (ORC) refers to professional shoplifting, cargo theft, retail crime rings and other organized crime occurring in the retail environments. According to National Retail Federation (NRF) statistics, 79 percent of retailers surveyed have said their company has been the victim of organized retail crime. Most of the merchandise stolen from retail stores is sold at flea markets, in the streets or through online auction sites. Statistics indicate that ORC is a $25 billion dollar a year business. Having a strategy to combat against this growing problem is essential. The best strategy is:

- Awareness
- Training
- Crime Data

It is well known that the best defense you can use against ORC is awareness. If not aggressively controlled, ORC rings have the potential to drastically impact your shortage. Knowledge on how they operate is the key to controlling your inventory losses. Most professional shoplifters operate in groups or teams and know the stores policies, associates and building layout. Armed with this detailed information of the store's operation, ORC groups are more able to successfully strike and steal undetected. Store management and associates need to be on the same page when identifying and preventing professional shoplifters. Once an ORC group has been identified, timing is very important in terms of immediate communication to the appropriate parties. Advising security or a manager in charge that you have a professional shoplifting group in the building will provide the best chance for making an apprehension and/or recovering the merchandise.

Receiving and understanding retail crime statistics and what it means is the key to stopping ORC. For example, seeing a trend of "grab and runs," where particular types of merchandise are taken at customer doors during a particular time and day, is very helpful when planning prevention.

APPREHENSION SAFETY

Anytime you make a shoplifting apprehension you

must first think about your own personal safety and that of your customers/employees. Following company rules and guidelines will decrease your chances of getting injured. Some shoplifters have a long and lengthy criminal history and will therefore resist, sometimes with violence, any attempt to apprehend them. There are many shoplifting apprehensions that have gone real bad because the store detective or someone from management was not properly trained and was hurt, while attempting to detain a suspected shoplifter. The industry's best practice advises you to have someone with you who has experience making apprehension and that you should also notify your local police department.

EXAMPLES OF METHODS TO ENSURE THE SAFETY OF YOURSELF AND THE SHOPLIFTER:

- Never get in an elevator with a shoplifter.
- While the shoplifter is in custody, never make disrespectful or demeaning comments

and always treat then them with respect.

- Never use excessive force during a shoplift-ing apprehension.

- Try not to make the apprehension alone. If possible, obtain assistance.

- When escorting the shoplifter, never allow the person to carry items that can be used to injure or hurt you.

- Remember, safety first at all times.

CUSTOMER SERVICE

This is a service-oriented industry and you must always take the position to do whatever is needed to assist your customers. You must remain calm and profes-sional in your duties and each decision you make must be accurate and in accordance with company policies and procedures. For example, many security associ-ates will have contact with customers during the open-ing and closing of the customer doors. During this time it is important to know that if customers ask to be let out of a particular door we must accommodate them. Listed in this section are a few tips for security associates to follow:

- Never have contact with a customer who is suspected of shoplifting, neither physical nor verbal, unless all five steps have been met and you are prepared to make an apprehension.

- If a customer stops you while you are performing routine floor surveillance, give them your complete attention.

- If a customer stops you while you are conducting a surveillance of a potential shoplifter, let them know you are security and politely refer them to a sales associate or manager.

Special note: Ticket Switching
Because of the legal complexities associated with
successfully proving a ticket-switching case in court
it is never advisable to make an apprehension based
on ticket switching. If a customer is observed switch-
ing tickets, security should instruct the sales associ-
ate at the register to verify the price of the item(s) in
question. If the customer then disputes the price, the
sales associate should treat the matter as a customer
service issue and involve a selling floor manager not
security.

BUSINESSES WITHOUT SECURITY PERSONNEL

In situations when there is no trained security associate in your building, and a customer shoplifts,
what do you do? You may have to ask an employee to make a tough decision such as approaching
the person and asking them if they would like to
pay for the items in the bag. This is not easy and
can place your business in a legally liable position
if not handled properly. The more information,
knowledge and training you have the more comfortable you will feel when placed in challenging
situations and when handling sensitive issues.

HELPFUL TIPS:

- Remember, safety first. Never physically place your hands on the customer.

- Always be pro-active. If you identify a cus-tomer in your store who is acting suspicious, approach them and offer customer service and increase awareness.

- When you approach the customer, you must always clearly identify yourself as an employ-ee of the company.

- Never accuse the customer of shoplifting. Politely ask the person if they would like to pay for the merchandise in their possession.

- If the customer refuses to give back mer-chandise they have not paid for, immedi-ately contact a supervisor and advise them of incident.

EMPLOYEE THEFT

It is common knowledge throughout the retail industry that employee theft is the number one shortage problem facing businesses and companies today. Employees have access to key areas and knowledge to circumvent policies and procedures. In many cases, they also know management and security personnel and their schedules. This information gives the associate an advantage and allows him or her to more effec-

tively deprive the company of assets. Pre/post employment screening and proper new hire training is a proactive measure to prevent employee dishonesty. Education and training on the different methods of employee theft is needed to identify associates who steal from the company. It is very important to know when and how to make an apprehension of a dishonest employee.

Here is a list of ways employees steal from companies and recommended ways to detect theft:

METHODS OF EMPLOYEE THEFT

- Cash theft from the register or co-workers.
- Merchandise theft
- Check fraud
- Fraudulent returns
- Gift Card fraud
- Credit Card fraud

Sources of Inventory Shrinkage

Shoplifting 31.60

Unknown 2.86

Admin & Vendor Error 23.75

Employee Theft 46.80

METHODS OF EMPLOYEE DETECTION

- Employee package inspection
- CCTV surveillance
- Confidential tips
- Point-Of-Sale (POS) exception reports
- Routine inspections of trash, garbage and compactors for merchandise being stashed for later theft

DIFFERENT TYPES OF EMPLOYEE THEFT

Account Returns:

1. Multiple returns processed by the same associate.

2. Associates returning merchandise to the same department where they are assigned.

3. Multiple returns during a short period of time.

4. Excessive "No Receipt" returns.

Third-party Bankcard Returns:

1. Multiple returns with the same dollar

amount or to the same department.

2. High concentration of returns in a short period of time.

3. Returns processed by the same associate.

4. Excessive "No Receipt" returns.

Cash/Mail/Merchandise
Certificate Returns:

1. Disproportionate number of returns processed by the same associate.

2. Frequency of high refunds issued to the same address and/or name

Voids:

1. High frequency of cash voids.

2. A gap between the transaction numbers to be voided and the actual void transaction number greater than five, or longer than fifteen minutes.

3. Void not followed by a new transaction.

4. Voids followed by a no-sale.

Account Purchases:

1. Obtaining merchandise by charging it to an unsuspecting customer's account.

2. Knowingly presenting an invalid card.

Stolen Bank Checks:

1. Purchase of merchandise.

2. Payment on an account to increase the Option to Buy.

Sales Associate Collusion:

1. The associate works with the fraud operator in order to commit the fraud.

2. Prior arrangements made to obtain fraudulent refunds, fraudulent exchanges, merchandise purchased with an invalid credit card and merchandise purchased with bad checks.

Fraudulent Bank Checks

In all suspected fraudulent bank check cases, store management should be contacted in order to determine the course of the investigation. Apprehensions for "bad checks" should only be made if the fraudulent nature of the case can be properly identified. In most cases, this requirement is very difficult to satisfy because of the limited time and the inability to verify the real owners of the checks.

Consequently, most companies utilize an automated check verification service to reduce their exposure at the point of sale. This service guarantees payment, provided the associate follows all of the proper check procedures.

Additional stolen check methods:

1. Stolen Checks: Use stolen checks to purchase merchandise.

2. Account Payments with Stolen Checks: Fraud Operator increases the losses on a stolen credit card by making payments to the account with stolen checks that increases the Open to Buy (OTB) credit limit.

3. Non-Sufficient Funds: Fraud Operator writes checks knowing that there is not enough money in the account to cover the cost of the merchandise. This is difficult to identify due to the lack of access to an individual's bank account.

4. Collusive Associate: Associate knowingly allows another associate to make purchases using stolen checks tendered for payment.

HELPFUL TIPS FOR PREVENTING EMPLOYEE THEFT

1. Thorough hiring process, background checks and training.

2. Proper management presence and supervision.

3. New associate orientation with a security representative or management explaining policy and discussing various methods of theft detection.

4. Comprehensive Point-of-Sale (POS) training and controls.

5. Regular inspections of associate packages and purchases. Consistency and regularity will discourage most associates from attempting to carry out stolen merchandise.

6. Inspect trash, garbage and compactors for merchandise being stashed for later theft.

7. Strict control over refund and void procedures.

8. Keeping watch over register terminals, credit, and cash operations.

9. Proper training in job responsibilities, policies and procedures. Highlighting accuracy in handling financial and sales documents.

10. Performing regular register audits.

11. Watching for associates who leave the store through unauthorized doors, with or without packages.

12. Learn retail store operations, merchandising, logistics and security policies and procedures.

13. Know cash handling rules, including becoming knowledgeable in operating a sales register. You will not be able to catch a dishonest associate who is manipulating the register for his or her own gain unless you understand the functions and vulnerabilities of the register.

14. Be attentive and alert to signs of policy non-compliance and be prepared to take disciplinary action.

15. Look for unusual circumstances or sudden/drastic changes in an associate's behavior.

16. Investigate cash losses, excessive voids (both mid-voids and post voids), no-sales, and refunds. Also, be aware of cash overages as they may be a sign of someone who is ringing fraudulent cash returns and either forgets or never gets the chance to remove the cash, thereby causing an overage.

SAFETY AWARENESS

CHAPTER 3
SAFETY AWARENESS

Occupational Safety Health Administration (OSHA) was founded in 1970 and has mandated that all businesses must provide a safe and healthy work environment for all employees and customers. Every business must adhere to federal rules and regulations regarding safety. In an effort to comply with all the OSHA rules and regulations, most companies will implement a safety program. Remember, a good safety program reduces claims, insurance premiums and net costs.

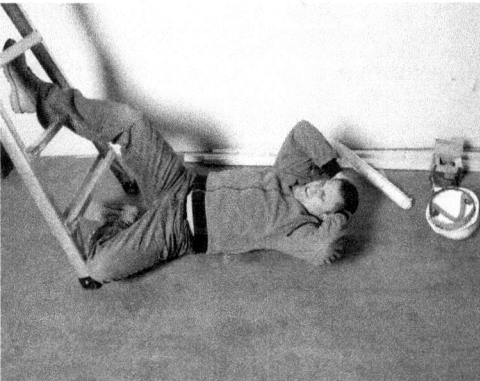

The goal of the program is to greatly improve safety conditions within the building. One of the best approaches is the formation of a safety committee to oversee the development and implementation of a safety program which maintains regulatory compliance, while enhancing and improving all safety disciplines. Some of the programs results should include an updated safety manual, increased safety training, and improved supervisor safety interventions. It is recommend that all employees and management attend safety training and comply with all the company's safety requirements. Safety issues should be discussed at scheduled employee meetings. Additionally, all employees are encouraged to make suggestions and stop any safety violation they observe. In today's retail industry security groups are now being held more accountable for reducing both workers compensation and general loss claims.

Included in your safety program should be the following:

- Bloodborne Pathogen Training
- CPR Training
- Building Fire Drills
- Elevator & Escalator Inspections
- Accident Reporting
- Safety Meetings
- Emergency Situations

BLOODBORNE PATHOGENS

Bloodborne pathogens are microorganisms in human blood that can cause disease. HBV and HIV are examples of bloodborne pathogens that you must be completely educated of in order to protect yourself. All companies are required to identify the employees at risk and provide training. Housekeeping and security are two groups that fall into this category and should receive specialized training.

CPR TRAINING

CPR (Cardiopulmonary Resuscitation) is a combination of rescue breathing (mouth-to-mouth resuscitation) and chest compressions. Most companies provide CPR training to their employees in case of an emergency. Employees should not attempt to administer CPR unless they are trained and certified.

BUILDING FIRE DRILLS

Fire drills and building evacuations must be conducted regularly. OSHA regulations are clear with regards to performing fire drills and building evacuations. The purpose is to ensure that our employees and customers know how to exit the building quickly and safely, in the event of a fire or smell of smoke. In addition, evacuation plans should be prominently displayed in employee entrances/exits; and fire exits should be signed and accessible.

ELEVATOR & ESCALATOR INSPECTIONS

Elevator and escalator inspections must be conducted daily to ensure that they are working properly prior to the start of business. All inspections must be recorded in a log and maintained in a safe place. If your elevator or escalator is not operating properly, you should call a technician for repairs immediately.

ACCIDENT REPORTING

Employee and customer accidents must be documented and reported to management. In addition to writing up an accident report, you should take photographs of the accident scene. The accident report and photos must be forwarded to management as soon as possible. Insurance carriers need all the accident information in order to handle an accident claim.

SAFETY MEETINGS

A proactive step that most companies utilize is to have monthly safety meetings to address safety issues. A certain number of associates with management are designated to meet and identify unsafe working conditions and take the necessary steps to address them with workable solutions.

EMERGENCY SITUATIONS

One of the most common misconceptions for sales associates or security is that handling emergency situations isn't their primary job function. Handling emergency situations is a significant part of the job because poorly handled emergencies can lead to a loss of property and human life. Every business should have an Emergency Preparedness Plan that addresses procedures and contact information for key personnel and emergency contacts. Copies of the Plan should be kept current and distributed to all relevant personnel. When responding to an emergency you must be prepared and know what actions you must take. The following are three emergency situations that are most concerning to businesses:

1. Fires that occur on your premises should be handled carefully. If the fire can be put out with an extinguisher, then do so. If not, call your local fire department. Never use water on an electrical fire.

2. Bomb threats have been an increasing concern after 9/11 and must be handled following your company's procedures. Always keep in mind that immediate notification to your local police department is your best course of action.

3. Power failures do happen. If you do not know what to do it could be costly for the company. In the event of a power failure, flashlights should be operational and accessible throughout the building. In addition,

all customer doors should be locked and

customers allowed to exit the premises.

INVENTORY CONTROL

CHAPTER 4
INVENTORY CONTROL

I nventory control of merchandise is a top priority for businesses, and will have a direct impact on profitability. Not having proper inventory control in place to track the flow of merchandise can adversely affect a company's ability to grow and be successful. Some companies use planners or buyers to purchase merchandise from vendors. They select different assortments based on customer trends and needs. An order is placed for goods and the merchandise is then shipped from the vendor to the distribution/logistics center or store location. At point of receipt, merchandise is accounted for into the inventory and then booked into the item file. The item file is an accounting system that calculates merchandise purchased, merchandise sold, and merchandised returned. At the distribution center, merchandise is then processed for distribution to the stores. We will now take a close look at different methods used in the industry for controlling inventory shortage that has been proven successful.

DISTRIBUTION CENTERS

Most retail companies operate a distribution or logistics center that handles all incoming merchandise from the vendors. These centers are designed for processing the flow of merchandise to and from the company. It is very important for production to the company's bottom line profit that the flow of goods and services are done correctly. Well-trained professionals should be working in the warehouse environment with very tight controls on the movement of goods, ticketing, and accuracy.

MOVEMENT OF GOODS

Movement of merchandise from the receiving platform to the selling floor can be a challenging process. If not handled properly the potential for loss is great. Merchandise delivered to the incorrect department can cause problems and can go uncounted for or stolen. Ensuring that all goods go to the correct area can be achieved by closely monitoring the movement from the receiving area to the final designation. It is highly recommended that you ensure that all paperwork is in order and signed off by the persons receiving the merchandise. After this is done you should make certain that all high shortage merchandise is properly stored.

STOCKROOMS

Well-organized stockrooms are a key to maintaining shortage control of merchandise. Stockroom doors should be kept closed and locked at all times to prevent intruders from entering and removing merchandise.

PRICE TICKET ACCURACY

It is very important for all sales associates to verify the price ticket information of the merchandise. All merchandise is ticketed with a control number or SKU, and in some cases, a barcode. The SKU numbers are used to identify the type of merchandise, price and track the items that are sold or returned.

MERCHANDISE PLACEMENT

Merchandise placement must always be consid-

ered when displaying goods. If desirable merchandise is placed too close to a customer door, it is highly likely that someone will steal it. Store merchants and security now work closely together on the placement of desirable merchandise. If it is determined that certain high profile goods must be placed in close proximity to a customer exit based on merchandise standards, then security/management must take the necessary precautions to secure and protect these items.

ELECTRONIC ARTICLE SURVEILLANCE SYSTEMS

Using all the current technology available to you is an important part of controlling inventory losses due to shoplifting. Electronic Article Surveillance (EAS) systems use a variety of tags, which are placed on the merchandise to prevent shoplifting. At the point of sale, an associate removes or deactivates the tag. If the tags are not removed or deactivated, an alarm will sound at the doors when a person attempts to exit.

INVENTORY COUNT

Due to the high price point of the merchandise, fine jewelry stores, for example, generally count all merchandise daily, sometimes twice a day. Knowing your company's procedure for merchandise handling is very important and recording your daily counts in a log is the only way to ensure you can reconcile properly. Retail stores that do not sell jewelry but have other desirable goods are also urged to count those items regularly and have merchandise movement strategies in place to track the goods from the receiving area to the selling floor.

STORE OPERATING STANDARDS

It is well known in the retail industry that if you do not adhere to the stores operating standards, you will incur shortages. For example, the sales associate does not close the fine jewelry case line door after servicing a customer. The customer can remove all the merchandise when the associate is not looking. Ensuring that merchandise is properly secured and stockroom doors are closed and locked are just a few examples of operating standards that one must follow.

AUDITING

In an effort to ensure that store-operating standards are maintained you should audit the store regularly. Management or security will check wrapstands, stockrooms, and showcases for compliance to operating standards. Most audits are graded and the results should quantify the work. The results should be reviewed with management and associates so the store can take action to correct all deficiencies. A re-audit should be conducted which gives the store and auditor a chance to see improvements.

FITTING ROOMS

Store fitting rooms must be kept neat and orderly at all times. If maintained properly, you will have the ability to quickly identify any evidence of theft activity. Regular inspections should be carried out routinely and a sign off sheet should be placed inside the area and signed once the inspection is completed. Your inspections should include looking for price tickets, defeated EAS tags and empty hangers. Associates should be aware of areas where tickets and tags could be easily concealed.

COMMUNICATIONS/ AWARENESS

CHAPTER 5
COMMUNICATIONS/AWARENESS

Research and experience has told us that you must have a high level of communication from the top of the management pyramid to the workforce in order to ensure that operating standards and shortage programs are executed. It is equally important that a flow of information and feedback is coming from the associates to upper management. In addition, shortage awareness is the most powerful, least costly and often neglected of all shortage measures. Shortage awareness is instilling a sense of ownership, protectiveness and involvement in the shortage awareness program among all employees. An effective communications program starts with awareness. Why is awareness at the top of the list of shortage prevention programs? It is common knowledge that a free and open flow of information pertaining to shortage causing events will prepare associates on what they need to do. If there is a new method of theft that is becoming more prevalent (i.e. organized retail crime) management must get that information out to the store population so they can help defend against it. If a company commits to forwarding all the necessary and important information out to their employee population it will make an impact on preventing shortages. Keep in mind that all communications must be accurate, consistent and target the entire store population, both full, day part time and night part time employees.

Listed below are some of the best practices within the retail industry:

- Store Rallies/AM and PM Meetings
- New Hire Orientation
- Company Satellite Communications
- Associate Meetings
- Awards Programs

- Contests

- Be-On-The-Look-out (BOLO)

STORE RALLIES/AM AND PM MEETINGS

One of the best methods for getting messages out about shortage is using store rallies or AM/PM meetings. Scheduling a storewide rally/meeting on a regular basis, generally before store opening, will give you an opportunity to communicate to a larger audience. Your shortage message should be quick and concise. Keeping your topics simple will ensure you capture the attention of your audience and the information is retained. Visual aids, such as a handful of price tickets or defeated EAS sensors recovered from a fitting room are also powerful tools. Videos and handouts are good vehicles to use as well.

COMPANY SATELLITE COMMUNICATIONS

Satellite communications give you the ability to broadcast to multiple locations from a central location. Making a satellite broadcast will require preparation and planning. Your preparation should start at least one month in advance with collecting all your materials and developing your script. On the day of shooting all preparation and planning should be complete.

ASSOCIATE MEETINGS

Conducting individual associate meetings with your store associates is also an effective way to get shortage messages out. Individual meetings are obviously very effective due to the direct nature of the communication, which allows for associate feedback. Your associates will usually retain the information longer if given an opportunity to ask questions.

AWARDS PROGRAMS

There is no better motivational tool for getting and keeping your associates involved in shortage retention and prevention than to use and promote an awards program. This program should be designed as an incentive for your associates to remain vigilant in calling out suspicious behavior. The awards can be given out in cash, gift cards, merchandise, credit, etc. It is recommended that the award should be a high enough value to remain a powerful incentive to your associates.

CONTESTS

Another way to get your associates to actively participate in the shortage program is to hold shortage awareness contests. These contests should be held on a consistent basis and should be aimed at getting your associates motivated towards reducing shortage. For example, you may want to conduct weekly contests for associates who call security/management to report suspicious customer behavior.

BE-ON-THE-LOOK-OUT (BOLOs)

BOLO's are a very common and effective way of delivering information regarding specific shoplifting groups or individuals who are targeting your company, as well as others, in a certain geographical location. This can be accomplished through emails and/or phone calls. A central database within your company that would allow you to download a photo image of the group or individuals responsible and then send this information out to other locations would be ideal. Keep in mind that if someone shoplifts from your store they will or have already shoplifted from another store close by. Establishing a network with neighboring stores will allow you to send and receive vital information within a short amount of time. Stores should use discretion when offering or receiving this information.

DIVERSITY AWARENESS

CHAPTER 6
DIVERSITY AWARENESS

I n the workplace there are differences among employees that can create unique challenges on the
job. It is strongly recommended that differences
between people should be used to benefit a company
not create division. Diversity, in simple terms, is a variety of factors that separate people from one another. It could be age, gender, race, color, socioeconomic
status, education, sexual orientation, ethnicity or so-
cial preference. Most successful companies are able
to use their employee's uniqueness to make the company stronger. There is a misconception that a diverse
workforce means having people from different ethnic
backgrounds. This is not what true workplace diversity
is all about. What you should be looking for in a diverse
workforce is people working with others with different
values, experiences, backgrounds, and preferences. It

is very important for workers to understand each others background and experiences. Acknowledging these differences and respecting each other will help make the workplace environment positive and productive.

- Manage Diversity in the Workplace
- Diversity Training
- Equal Rights in the Workplace

The first step in managing group diversity is being aware of potential problems. The manager must be present in the workplace often enough to notice problems. He or she must also be available for discreet complaints, either from victims or concerned onlookers.

Education is another key step in managing a diverse workplace. Each employee is instructed in what constitutes harassment, abuse or intolerable behavior. One man's joke is another man's "hostile environment." Requiring employees to take these classes may detract from productivity but they are still cheaper than hiring lawyers to represent you in a lawsuit.

All employees are entitled to be treated fairly and with respect. The equal rights laws are governed by the Equal Employment Opportunity Commission (EEOC). Some practices that are considered discriminatory are:

RACIAL PROFILING

It must be clearly communicated to all company employees that racially profiling customers is not only against company policy, but also is a violation of Federal law. Sales associates on the floor who lack diversity training and make an assumption based on appearances commit the majority of racial profiling in department stores. Anti racial profiling training should not be limited to store management and security, but to the entire store population. However it is store management's responsibility to hire sales associates and security personnel, and provide training on how to detect shoplifters while not racially profiling minorities. Based on studies of racial profiling it is known that most minorities who have experienced racial profiling while shopping never reported it or believe it to be typical in society. In this chapter, we will review the following best practices in avoiding racial profiling.

- Anti-Racial Profiling Training
- Suspicious Customer Behavior
- Methods for Identifying, and Monitoring Employees Who Racially Profile

If you are to make an impact within your company to stop racial profiling, you need to first educate and train all store personnel. Training on what constitutes suspicious customer behavior is important. Listed are some behaviors that may indicate suspicious activity by a customer:

1. Enters the store repeatly without making a purchase. Appears to be nervous while selecting merchandise.
2. Watches the sales associate more than shopping.
3. Unusual walking with small steps which may indicate they have concealed merchandise.
4. Wears bulky clothes or attire out of season.

Retail security personnel have been trained to use information from apprehension records as a tool to narrow the field of possible suspects. Using data obtained from inventory results, apprehension statistics, merchandise shortage reports, security can develop a profile of a shoplifter. The profile can tell you what type of merchandise, what day of the week, what time of day, and what department will have the most shoplifting activity. Using this information to help pinpoint a shoplifter is totally acceptable as long as it is not used to racially profile.

Suspicious behavior displayed by customers helps security focus on the right people. What is suspicious behavior? Some other behaviors can be categorized as customers not looking at the price tickets, watching the sales associates, frequently looking up at the cameras, or rapidly selecting large quantities of merchandise. If these indicators are observed, you must alert security and/or management. If you are alone, then ask him or her if they need assistance in an attempt to prevent theft. Companies have been challenged to develop programs that can be used to help identify employees who unknowingly racially profile. In most cases security has been instructed to al-

ways ask the person calling to report a suspicious customer to explain what the customer is doing. By asking the question it makes your associates think about what is suspicious behavior. Additionally, mystery shoppers have been challenged to test associates and security on whether they racially profile customers.

WORKPLACE VIOLENCE

CHAPTER 7
WORKPLACE VIOLENCE

Workplace violence can be any act of physical violence, threats of physical violence, harassment, intimidation, or other threatening, disruptive behavior that occurs at the workplace. Workplace violence can affect or involve employees, visitors or contractors. A number of actions in the work environment can trigger or cause workplace violence. It may even be the result of non-work-related situations such as domestic violence or "road rage." Workplace violence can be inflicted by an abusive employee, a manager, supervisor, co-worker, customer, family member, or even a stranger. Whatever the cause or whoever the perpetrator, workplace violence is not to be tolerated. In today's society workplace violence is no longer a hidden secret and most management personnel have been trained on how to handle violence at the workplace. Quick early detection of individuals who may be capable of violence on the job is the first step to preventing it. Having a workplace violence plan is very important and is very cost effective. Listed are some suggested programs that will help prevent workplace violence.

- Pre/Post-Employment Screening
- On-site Security
- Awareness Training
- Emergency Plan

In an effort to prevent hiring employees who may eventually become violent if their hot button is pushed, it is recommended that all new hires go through pre-employment screening. Due diligent background checks will include, but not limited to, criminal history, address verification, and references. Also, pre-employment assessment testing with specific questions that help to identify potential problem employees.

A highly visible and well-trained security department and management team is deterrence against most workplace violence.

VIOLENCE AGAINST EMPLOYEES

Businesses should be alert to the risk of robbery coupled with criminal assaults on their employees. To address this danger, each business should have an established workplace violence prevention plan and train employees in measures to prevent these crimes and to protect their safety. Your first consideration is to apply preventive measures in your workplace. These preventive measures include engineering and practice controls. Engineering controls decrease or remove the hazard from the workplace or create a barrier between the worker and the hazard. Administrative and work practice controls describe procedures and practices that can help prevent violent incidents. Examples are: adequate staffing, training, or security personnel. Your second consideration is to develop an emergency plan of action. Ensure that employees know emergency phone numbers and other necessary information. Discuss emergency procedures: Is there a panic button? Do employees have distinct tasks during an emergency?

Special Note: It is important that security, human resource and legal partnerships are maintained consistently after any incident.

PROFESSIONAL ETHICS
AND CONDUCT

CHAPTER 8

PROFESSIONAL ETHICS & CONDUCT

Strickland Security & Safety Solutions will maintain our values of morality, ethics and integrity. Anyone who attends our workshop/seminar should embrace the code of honesty and ethics. All retail companies and businesses should have some form of business code of conduct. Why is it important for every company to have some form of a business code of ethics? For starters our society is one in which legation is high and companies that do not have the appropriate procedures and policies in place will have a hard time defending allegations of wrong doing or failing to comply with federal non discriminatory standards. Most companies' core values start with being honest, fair and operating with integrity. As an associate you must review and understand the significance of complying with your company's business code of ethics. Complete understanding of all company ethics and conduct policies and following them is the first step needed toward having a healthy working environment for all employees. A positive working atmosphere will help improve productivity and decrease workplace confrontation and conflict. In an effort to assist you with achieving this goal you should clearly understand all the following components.

- General Conduct
- Anti-Racial Profiling
- Excessive Force
- Pursuit of Suspects
- Confidentiality
- Customer Incidents
- Testifying in Court

GENERAL CONDUCT

Every company/business should have a general code of conduct for their employees to read, sign and abide by.

Sample:

"I acknowledge that after I complete my requirements for training that I will adhere to the highest standards of my profession. My job security will depend on me following the professional business code of conduct. I fully realize that failure to perform my duties within the letter and spirit of the business code of conduct or any misconduct may lead to disciplinary action up to and including termination of employment from the company that employs me. I realize that I must respect the basic civil rights of all employees, customers and shoplifters, regardless of race, sex, religion, color, national origin, citizenship or sexual orientation. Sexual harassment of any kind toward customers, shoplifters, or company employees is strictly prohibited."

ANTI-RACIAL PROFILING

Security professionals are expected to respect the civil rights of all customers and employees of the company. Initiating a surveillance of a customer or employee based on race, skin color, sex, religion, or national origin will not be tolerated. All observations of customers and employees will only be based on suspicious behavior. Racial profiling is a violation of federal law and against the business code of conduct.

SAMPLE:

"I fully acknowledge that I have read and understood all the policies relating to anti-racial profiling, violation of these policies will lead to disciplinary action up to and including loss of employment."

EXCESSIVE FORCE

The use of unwarranted and unnecessary force against customers or shoplifters is a serious violation of company policy and will not be tolerated. Using more force than is required to detain a shoplifter or employee can lead to serious injury or death. The use of excessive force can cause a company liability and the apprehending person civil accountability as well. If a person apprehended for theft is unable to be detained without using excessive force, the apprehension must be aborted immediately.

PURSUIT OF SUSPECTS

It is highly recommended not to pursue a shoplifter off of company property. Shoplifters who exit the building with stolen merchandise and cannot be apprehended within a reasonable distance should not be followed or pursued.

CONFIDENTIALITY

It is imperative that all employees refrain from engaging in "gossip" or repeating sensitive information to people uninvolved in the situation. Defamation of character occurs when you report confidential information which injures a person's reputation.

CUSTOMER INCIDENTS

All customer incidents or threats of civil action against the company must be reported immediately to management or supervisor in charge.

TESTIFYING IN COURT

Testifying honestly in a court of law and utilizing professional and ethical guidelines are necessary if you are ever summoned to testify on behalf of the company. Dress code, writing skills, providing accurate information and telling the truth are all so very important.

TERMS & DEFINITIONS

ACCOMPLICE: A person who knowingly, voluntarily, and with common intent with the principle offender, unites in the commission of a crime. In order to be considered an accomplice to a theft in, the person must have physically participated in the theft act. "Blocking" or acting as a "shield" does not satisfy our definition of an accomplice.

ACCOUNTABILITY: The state of being responsible or answerable for one's actions or failures to act. Documentation creates an audit trail for accountability.

AD: "Administrative Discharge" (AD). Term used to describe the termination of an Associate for violation of one or more a company's policies or rules of conduct. Does not infer criminal activity, as opposed to "DE".

ADMISSION: A statement by a subject from which guilt may be inferred, but only tending to prove the offense charged, and not amounting to a confession.

AFFIDAVIT: A sworn, written statement, made voluntarily, taken before an officer having authority to administer such an oath. (See "Deposition")

APPREHENSION: The seizure, taking, or arrest of a person on a criminal charge.

ARBITRATION: Process of resolving a disputed matter before a private, non-judicial person. Arbitration may occur either by agreement of the parties to dispute or, in some instances, be provided for by law.

ASSAULT: Any willful attempt or threat to inflict injury to another person, when coupled with the apparent ability to do so, and any intentional display of force that would give the victim reason to fear or expect immediate bodily harm. An assault may be committed without actually touching, or striking, or doing bodily harm to another person. Some states require actual physical injury to have taken place. Refer to individual state law for details.

ASSAULT AND BATTERY: Any willful touching of another, which is without justification or excuse.

AUDIT: A formal or official examination, and /or verification of a financial or operating area.

BANDIT BARRIER: Interlocking set of bulletproof doors designed to limit unauthorized access to the cash office or vault room.

BATTERY: Any willful physical contact of some sort (i.e., bodily injury or offensive touching of another person).

BOOSTER BOX: A box with a spring-loaded end used for shoplifting. Variations include booster girdles, booster coats and other garments or devices specifically designed to aid shoplifters in concealing stolen merchandise.

CASH VARIANCE: A difference, a discrepancy between cash transactions recorded on the register and actual cash on hand.

CCTV: "Closed Circuit Television" Surveillance cameras and monitors used to observe specific areas. May be used concealed ("covert") or in open view as a deterrent. Some camera domes are equipped with red flashing lights as a greater deterrent.

CHAIN OF CUSTODY: The sequence of persons who have actual possession and/or control over a physical object that is to be used as evidence at a trial.

CIVIL DEMAND / CIVIL RECOVERY: Terms used interchangeably; referring to laws in some states that provide for merchants to assess shoplifters with financial penalties based on the value of the merchandise involved. The laws are intended to deter shoplifting while partially reimbursing retailers for the costs associated with providing assets protection.

CIVIL LAW: That division of law that is occupied with the enforcement of civil rights, as distinguished from criminal law. Personal injury lawsuits and divorces are civil cases. Theft, robbery or burglary cases are criminal.

CODE OF CONDUCT: A collection of rules relating to the behavior and conduct of all Security Associates. All company Associates must sign this form upon being hired, and annually thereafter. Any violation of the Code of Conduct can result in disciplinary action up to and including termination of employment.

COLLUSION: A secret agreement or cooperation for an illegal or deceitful purpose.

COMPLAINT: In civil law, it is the first or initial pleading on the part of the plaintiff. A complaint gives the defendant information on all material facts on which the plaintiff relies to support his/her case.

CONSENT SEARCH: A search conducted pursuant to a voluntary agreement, either verbally or in writing.

CONCEALMENT: The act of hiding something so that it is not visible through ordinary observation.

CONFESSION: A voluntary statement of guilt by a person who has committed a crime.

CONTRABAND: Any weapon, illegal drugs or other illegal item in the possession of an apprehended person.

COOP: Also known as a perch, booth or lookout. A concealed enclosure from which security personnel can observe an area or an activity.

CRIME: Any act committed or omitted in violation of the criminal laws of the State. These acts or omissions are classified as misdemeanors and felonies.

CRIMINAL: One who has committed a criminal offense and has been legally convicted of a crime.

CRIMINAL ACTION: An action prosecuted by the State against a person charged with committing a public criminal offense. A criminal action may be started when a citizen files a charge. (When a security representative signs a criminal complaint on behalf of their company against a shoplifter or a dishonest employee, the security representative is actually initiating a citizen complaint.) It is then that the State becomes the prosecuting party. Every criminal action will have the State or Commonwealth versus the party accused of committing the crime. Therefore, a prosecutor or district attorney, acting on behalf of the State or Commonwealth, ultimately makes all decisions regarding the prosecution of criminal cases in the courts.

CRIMINAL INFORMATION OR COMPLAINT: The document commencing a criminal action, brought by an appropriate officer of the State without consideration by a Grand Jury.

CRIMINAL LAW: That branch or division of law that treats crimes and their punishment.

CRIMINAL TRESPASS: The act of being in or entering a place unlawfully.

CROSS EXAMINATION: The questioning of a witness by the opposing attorney following direct examination. When a Security representative testifies for the prosecution, the initial questioning by the prosecutor/district attorney is called a "direct exam" and the follow-up questioning by the defense attorney is called a "cross exam." After that, the prosecutor can question the witness again, and that's called a "re-direct," and the defense attorney can follow up with a "re-cross."

CUSTOMER PICK-UP: The area designated in each store for holding customer purchases that are too large or bulky to carry out of the building by hand. Customers present their receipts to claim their purchases.

DE: "Dishonest Employee" (DE) is a designation applied to an Associate who commits a criminal act with intent to defraud the company regardless of whether or not the Company actually incurs a loss. This includes, but is not limited to, the theft of merchandise, theft of cash, credit fraud, and return fraud.

DEFALCATION: An act of embezzlement. The act of converting to one's own uses the property of another, over which the perpetrator has control, but not title or ownership interest.

DEFAMATION OF CHARACTER: Injuring a person's character, fame or reputation by false or malicious statements given to a third party. These statements can be either written ("libel") or spoken ("slander"). An example would be someone crying out, "Stop, Thief." That is why people who have been detained are called "suspects" and must be handled with respect until the court determines their innocence or guilt.

DEFENDANT: The party summoned to answer a charge or complaint, which may be a civil or criminal action. The person or entity against which a complaint or criminal action is brought.

DEPOSITION: A sworn, written statement made by a witness to be used as testimony in court. A deposition contains testimony, whereas an affidavit contains a statement.

DETACHER: A device used to remove an Electronic Article Surveillance (EAS) tag from merchandise. Detachers can be electronic or manual. A "Deactivator" merely disarms the EAS tag without physically removing it from the merchandise.

DETAIN: To stop, hold, delay or keep; to restrain from proceeding; in or as if in custody.

DETENTION: A period of temporary custody. The only time a Security person is authorized to detain a customer is when he and/or other members of the Security Department have witnessed the customer commit "shoplifting"

DIRECT EXAMINATION: The questioning of a witness called by a party in its own behalf during the course of a hearing, deposition or trial.

DISPOSITION: The settlement of an individual's case. When an executive "dispositions" a case, he/she either makes a decision to prosecute (turn the individual over to the police and file a formal criminal charge) or to release (let the person go, without involving the police or the courts).

DISBURSEMENT: Funds paid out for authorized expenditures.

DISCREPANCY: A difference, a variance.

DITCH: The act of discarding merchandise within the store that was taken with the intent to shoplift prior to an apprehension. Also called a "dump."

DOCUMENTATION: The act of furnishing, providing or authenticating with documents.

DUE PROCESS: A course of legal proceedings according to rules and principles that have been established in our legal system for the enforcement and protection of private rights. It implies the right of a person to be present before a judge, and to be able to provide testimony, or to otherwise defend his/her position.

DUMP: When a shoplifter drops or discards concealed, unpaid for merchandise to avoid apprehension; also called a "ditch."

EAS: Electronic Article Surveillance. A system using special tags affixed to merchandise which, when passed through an electromagnetic field, will cause a signal (audible alarm).

FAILURE-TO-REMOVE (FTR): The failure of a sales associate to properly detach or deactivate an EAS tag from a customer's purchase at the point of sale. FTR's are the most common cause for EAS signals at the exits, and this is the reason why Security and sales associates should always respond to EAS signals assuming that the signal is the result of an error by the a sales associate, as opposed to an attempted theft by the customer.

FALSE ARREST: Any unlawful physical restraint of another's liberty. A "false arrest" charge in a civil law suit alleges that the plaintiff (the person bringing the lawsuit) was falsely and illegally detained or otherwise had their freedom of movement unlawfully restricted. Security personnel can avoid making apprehension mistakes that may result in "false arrest" lawsuits by simply following your company's guidelines

FALSE IMPRISONMENT: The unlawful detention of a person for any length of time whereby he/she is deprived of his/her personal liberty. False imprisonment may take place without the actual application of any physical restraints like locks or bars, but by verbal compulsion and the display of available force. False imprisonment can be alleged even when movements are restrained on an open street. The imprisonment need not be for an appreciable length of time or cause damage to the person. Once you have detained Someone, the burden of proof is on you to show legal justification ("probable cause") for having detained the person.

FALSIFICATION: To misrepresent, to make false, by mutilation or addition or deletion. For example, a person who falsifies his employment application by failing to list a previous employer which he believes may furnish a bad reference, has "falsified" a Company document. Such falsification is subject to disciplinary action up to and including termination of employment.

FELONY: A crime of a more serious nature than a misdemeanor, often punishable by large fines and incarceration in a penitentiary or county jail.

FIVE STEPS RULE: A list of five separate and distinct steps that must be observed before a security associate is authorized to make an apprehension of a customer for the act of shoplifting. If any of the steps are not 100% satisfied, the Security representative must not apprehend. A willful violation of this rule will result in termination of the Security representative's employment.

GRAB AND RUN/ SNATCH AND GRAB: A method of shoplifting. The thief grabs an armload of merchandise and, with no attempt to conceal it, runs out of the building, usually into a waiting car.

GRAND JURY: A body of citizens impaneled to determine if "probable cause" exists that a particular crime was committed and that a specific individual committed it. This is not a determination of the ultimate guilt or innocence of the person involved, but rather a determination that the individual should be held for a trial.

GUILTY, PLEA OR FINDING: Confession of guilt made by a defendant in open court; or a finding made by a judge or jury at the conclusion of a criminal or civil trial.

HANDOUT: The act of an associate passing money and/or unpaid for merchandise to another individual. Also called a "pass off" or a "sweetheart deal."

HOLDUP BUTTON: A device used to create a silent alarm signal to alert the alarm company and police that a holdup is in progress. These devices are direct-wired to alarm company and are used in high security areas such as the cash office and fine jewelry. The same type of device may be used as a "Disturbance Button" which does NOT send a signal to the alarm company. Disturbance buttons send signals strictly within a company usually to a Security office or communications center, and are used to alert Security about customer disturbances or other non-holdup incidents requiring an immediate response by Security personnel.

IMPOSTOR: Someone represents themselves as another person: common in credit fraud cases.

INDICTMENT: The formal written charge issued by a Grand Jury when it determines that there is a probable cause to believe that a crime has been committed and that a specific individual has committed it.

INVENTORY: Generic name for the total merchandise on hand in the store; the physical counting of merchandise to compare to records ("book stock") and determine "shortage."

JURISDICTION: The power conferred upon a court by law, by which it is authorized to hear and determine a cause. The locale or area over which a particular court presides.

JURY TRIAL: Trial before ordinary citizens selected according to law and presided over by a judge. In a jury trial, the jury decides questions of fact. The judge rules on questions of law and maintains close supervision over the conduct of the trial. The number of jurists depends on the type of crime or offense and the laws of each state.

LAW: A set of rules enacted by the legislature and enforced by the police through the courts, regulating the ways in which people and businesses operate. State laws may differ greatly from state to state. Federal laws apply across all states. An example of a federal law is "Mail Fraud" which is the use of the U.S. Mail to commit a fraud, such as submitting a falsified credit application. An "ordinance" is similar to a law, but is enacted at a local or municipal/city level, and is enforceable only within the jurisdiction of the city or municipality.

LIBEL: A malicious defamation expressed in writing, printing, etc. The oral version of this is called "slander."

LOOKOUT: A booth, perch or coup which security personnel use to make covert observations, usually of the selling floor, for the purpose of detecting thefts.

MALICIOUS PROSECUTION: A legal term referring to the prosecution of a person when there was no "probable cause" to believe that the person actually committed the crime for which they were prosecuted. A company may be charged with malicious prosecution whenever a court has dismissed a case we initiated, or the alleged shoplifter has been found "not guilty" by a court.

MEDIA: All paperwork used in processing sales transactions, including the journal role, copies of sales checks, refunds, voids, and cash receipts.

MERCHANDISE MOVEMENT LOG: A receiving form which is filled out when Security merchandise (high value merchandise) is moved from a Security cage, receiving platform or other area to the selling floor. The selling floor representative, signifying the receipt of the merchandise and the transfer of possession and responsibility for safeguarding the merchandise, should sign the form.

MISDEMEANOR: An offense defined by law as less serious than a felony, and generally punishable by a fine or jail sentence of less than one year.

MISSING MERCHANDISE REPORT (MMR): A Security report form used to document a loss, presumably by theft, of salable merchandise. (Formerly referred to as a Known Shortage Report.)

M.O.: Method of Operation. The method that a shoplifter or dishonest employee uses to commit a theft.

NEW-HIRE: A person who has been recently employed by a company

NOT GUILTY, PLEA OR FINDING: A denial of guilt by a defendant in open court; or, a pronouncement of innocence by a judge or jury at the conclusion of a criminal or civil trial.

NO SALE: A transaction rung on a register that opens the register drawer without recording an actual financial transaction. Dishonest employees often use "no sales" to commit thefts of cash from the register.

NOLO CONTENDRE: Literally, a plea of "no contest" to a criminal charge. For practical purposes, it has the same effect as a guilty plea.

OATH: The formal affirmation by a person that he/she will act faithfully and tell the truth. Violation of this oath in the context of a court proceeding (i.e., failure to tell the truth when providing sworn testimony) constitutes the crime of perjury.

OBJECTION: In the course of a trial, the assertion that a specific question put to a witness is improper, either in form or substance. Objections may also be made to the introduction into evidence of physical objects, including records and documents.

OVERRULE: In the course of a trial, the determination by the judge that the legal basis for an objection is insufficient, and that the question must be answered or the physical evidence must be admitted. Opposite of "sustain."

PALMING: The concealment of small items (cash or merchandise) in a shoplifter's hand. This type of concealment is common with dishonest employees stealing money from the register, and shoplifters stealing fashion jewelry.

PASS-OFF: Same as "Hand-Out."

PAT-DOWN: A cursory search of the person for the sole purpose of discovering and removing offensive weapons. This is the only type of search Security personnel are authorized to conduct, and persons of the same gender must perform them.

PERJURY: The act of willfully testifying falsely under oath.

PLAINTIFF: The person or entity that initiates a legal action seeking damages, sanctions or other relief from the courts.

PLATFORM: The "dock" area in a building where trucks deliver and pick up shipped merchandise.

PLEA: In a criminal case, an agreement reached between the prosecution and defense, with the approval of the judge, to reduce the charges and/or recommend a specific sentence in exchange for a guilty plea.

P.O.S.: Point of sale.

PRELIMINARY HEARING: In a criminal action, a hearing before a judge to determine whether there is "probable cause" to go forward with a trial or to refer the matter to a Grand Jury.

PRICE NEGOTIATION: Term used to describe an unauthorized reduction in the price of merchandise agreed upon by a dishonest sales associate and customer.

PROBABLE CAUSE: A requisite element of a valid search and seizure or arrest. Probable Cause refers to a collection of existing facts and circumstances within one's knowledge, and of which one has reasonably trustworthy information, which are sufficient in themselves to warrant a person of reasonable caution to believe that a crime has been committed (in the context of an arrest) or that property subject to seizure is at a Designated location (in the context of a search and seizure).

PROMISSORY NOTE: A promise, in writing, to pay a specified sum at or during a specified time. The equivalent of a contract that a dishonest employee signs acknowledging past thefts and promising to repay the company for its losses.

PROSECUTION: In criminal law, an action or proceeding instituted and carried on before a court, for the purpose of determining the guilt or innocence of a person charged with a crime.

PROSECUTING ATTORNEY, PROSECUTOR: The attorney who presents evidence in the name of the government, against a criminal defendant. One who instigates a prosecution by making an affidavit charging a named person with the commission of a crime, on which a warrant is issued or an indictment or accusation is based. Also known in some jurisdictions as the "D.A." (District Attorney) or "A.D.A." (Assistant District Attorney).

READING THE REGISTER: Totaling the sales transactions and cash processed.

REASONABLE FORCE: The amount of force that a reasonable person would describe as just, suitable, moderate and tolerable under the circumstances -- force that is not excessive, overwhelming, brutal, unnecessary or unreasonable. The amount of force that a Security person must employ in order to protect himself and others from injury while attempting to apprehend a suspect, must be determined on the basis of the individual circumstances at the time. However, these basic ground rules apply in all situations: Security personnel may never use more or greater force than reasonably appears to be necessary under the circumstances to prevent bodily injury to themselves or anyone else. If there is ever reason to believe that there is a strong likelihood of physical injury occurring to anyone as a result of attempting to make an apprehension then the apprehension should not be made. The Security person should attempt to prevent or discourage the theft and recover the stolen property, while permitting the shoplifter to leave.

RECEIVING: An area within each store in which all merchandise is delivered, checked and distributed to the proper departments.

RECONCILE: To settle or balance. "Reconciliation" is a period of days in which stores attempt to discover and correct errors contributing to inventory shortage.

REFUNDER: A person who returns merchandise for cash or credit. Refunding in itself is not a crime; however, shoplifters will commonly steal and return merchandise as if they had bought it. That, of course, is a crime and is usually called "obtaining money (or credit) under false pretenses" and falls under the general heading of "fraud." Suspected refunders making returns without proof of purchase, should be given Mail MOC's (mail refunds) as opposed to In-Store MOC's. This will allow Security the opportunity to cancel the refund if an investigation warrants.

REPORT OF INVESTIGATION: Security form used to document the details of an investigation, apprehension or other Security-related incident.

RESTITUTION: The act of making good or giving any equivalent for any loss, damage or injury. Most commonly, it means paying back the amount owed from previous thefts. This is not to be confused with "recovery." Recoveries refer to the cash or merchandise recovered at the time of the apprehension, whereas restitution is money owed or paid for past thefts which were not recovered.

SEARCH: To examine the person or property of another person in an attempt to locate certain items or property. A "pat down" is the only type of search of the person that Security personnel are authorized to perform.

SEIZURE: The taking of possession of the property of another person.

SHOPLIFTING: The act of taking merchandise from a store without paying for it. Although the precise definitions vary from state to state, the basic elements are:
- Shoplifting is larceny, which is commonly called theft.
- Theft is the taking or carrying away of the property of another without the consent of the owner, or when the consent is obtained by fraud or coercion.
- The shoplifter has the intent to permanently deprive the owner of the value of the property.

SHORTAGE: The difference between the book stock and the physical inventory. Also defined as "shrink" or "loss".

SLANDER: An oral statement impeaching the honesty, integrity, virtue or reputation of an individual with malicious intent. The written version of slander is called "libel."

SLEEP-IN: A person found sleeping or roaming about inside a location after regular business hours. Also defined as a "Stay-In."

SMALL CLAIMS COURT: Civil courts of limited jurisdiction, generally organized so that parties may present cases without the need for attorneys. The rules of evidence and civil procedure are usually simplified.

SMASH AND GRAB: A particular form of burglary. The distinctive characteristics are speed and surprise. It involves smashing a barrier, usually a display window in a shop or a showcase, grabbing valuables and then making a quick getaway. There is no concern for setting off alarms or creating noise.

STATE'S CASE: In a criminal action, the prosecuting attorney or plaintiff is the State, not the complainant, (i.e., a Security associate signs a criminal complaint for shoplifting on behalf of a company but the State is the actual complainant on behalf of its citizens.)

SUBPOENA: A court document requiring a witness to appear at a certain place and time to give testimony before a court or magistrate, or in the form of a deposition. Subpoenas can also be for records and documentation (see below). Refusal to comply with a subpoena may result in penalties being imposed against the witness for contempt of court, resulting in fines and/or imprisonment.

SUBPOENA DUCES TECUM: A court document requiring a person or company to produce records or other written material. The penalty for refusal to comply is the same as described above.

SUMMONS: A legal document requiring a defendant to appear in court at a specific time and place to answer a suit or other legal charge that has been brought against him/her.

SUSTAIN: A ruling by a judge supporting an objection to a question put to a witness or the introduction of evidence. If an objection to a question is sustained, the witness should not answer the question. Opposite of "overrule."

SWITCHED TICKET: A customer switches price tickets on two items for the purpose of trying to purchase the more expansive item at the cheaper price.

TESTIFY: To give oral evidence as a witness under oath in response to questions by counsel.
Testimony: Evidence given by a witness under oath.

TILL TAP: When cash is stolen from a register.

UNDER-RING: Selling merchandise at less than the authorized retail price.

UPC: Unit Price Code. A 12-digit number specifically issued for a piece of merchandise, describing the item's color, style, etc.

VAULT: An area within a store that houses money and processes financial transactions; also called "Cash Room."

VERDICT: The decision of a jury (e.g., "Guilty" or "Not Guilty").

VISUAL SECURITY OFFICER (VSO): A highly visible, uniformed security associate who is dedicated to patrol or "cover" a customer entrance/exit or a high-shortage/high-theft area within a store.

VOID: The act of canceling a document or a sales transaction.

WARRANT: A writ issued by a judge requiring peace officers to perform certain acts. A search warrant allows police to search a premise or vehicle for specific physical or documentary evidence. An arrest warrant requires police to arrest an individual and bring them before a court to answer legal charges. A "Bench Warrant" is an arrest warrant issued by a judge, usually for a defendant who failed to appear in a criminal proceeding as summoned.